Sonnet, Sonnet, What's in Your Bonnet?

Sherry Roberts

Published by Pen It Publications in the U.S.A.
713-526-3989
www.penitpublications.com

ISBN: 978-1-63984-420-3

Sonnet, Sonnet, what's in your bonnet?

All the flowers my garden grows.

Zinnias, daylilies, and sunflowers galore.

Tulips, crocus, and daisies, too.

Come see the flowers my garden grows.

Here are the Zinnias in so many colors.

Some have beautiful crowns in their center.

Others have petals that fill out so full.

Look in my bonnet at this blanket flower.

Their name comes from the color design of their petals.

It looks like a Native American blanket.

The flower crowns, or centers, provide food for birds to nibble.

A bed of bachelor buttons in pinks, blues,
and purples share their colors for all to see.

I will fill my bonnet with so much color.

Here is a favorite bed of mine.
It is filled with sunflowers of all sizes and colors.
They follow the sun as it rises and sets.
There are tall giants that reach for the sky.
And a fun smaller size known as Teddy Bears.

Did you know sunflowers can also be found in colors of mahogany, bronze, and gold?

There is even a sunflower called Chocolate Cherry.

The flowers can be harvested for the seeds.

Sunflower seeds are a favorite of my bird friends, too.

In some cultures, sunflowers are a symbol of courage.

Here are my happy blooms!
I like to make a daisy chain or simply make a wish.

Make a wish with me:
"I wish yes." Pull a petal.
"I wish no." Pull a petal.

The last petal will tell you if your wish comes true if you end on yes, or not, if you end on no.

Oh, the beauty of daylilies fill my bonnet with colors galore!

Daylily blooms can have such a variety, and they can grow in sun or shade.

Every day they have a new bloom to share, many from summer until fall.

Look in my bonnet at this little flower. Although it has lily as part of its name, it is actually in the iris family.

It is known as a blackberry lily or leopard lily. It gets the name leopard lily because of the spots on the blooms that look like a leopard's fur.

Blackberry lilies attract nectar-drinking birds such as hummingbirds.

It is fun to fill my bonnet with irises.
Iris of purples, whites, yellows, and more,
bloom spring, summer, and some into fall.

The name for this flower comes from the
Greek word for rainbow.

Since irises come in colors of the rainbow,
this is a good name for this flower.

Sonnet shows you another member of the iris family, the crocus.

In the very early spring, one variety peeks up through the snow laden ground.

Colors of yellow, pink, purple, and white can be seen.

These are the shortest of the iris family. They grow only 2-5 inches in height.

The tulips also herald in the spring,
With bright colors of red, white, pink, yellow, and more.

Although The Netherlands in Europe is the primary producer of tulips,
they can also grow on farms in North Central and Northwest America.

In some cultures, a red tulip is the declaration of love.

Each spring, my bonnet is filled with daffodils. Their blooms come in yellow to white, with ruffle centers, too.

In Wales, the daffodil is the national flower.

Did you know there are festivals around the world as the daffodils announce spring?

Can you smell the sweet fragrance of this flower?

It is a hyacinth and fills my bonnet also in the spring.

In a variety of colors with red, pink, blue, purple, orange, white and yellow.

This beautiful flower grows a long, thick stem with many flowers on one stem.

Coneflowers, or echinacea, have cone-head shaped centers with petals that point downward.

This flower was used by Native American people as part of their folk medicines.

Bees, butterflies, and small birds like to feed off these beautiful flowers.

I like to grow these in clusters to add dots of color in my garden.

Sonnet, Sonnet asks what's in your bonnet?

Plant a garden no matter the size
and watch all the flowers grow.

Share them with friends both old and new,
as you build a garden... just for you.

About the Author

Sherry Roberts is an award-winning children's book author. Creating has always been a life-long adventure for her and making up stories stimulates this creativity. With three nieces and one nephew, she would make-up stories to entertain them. Over the last several years, she began to write picture books. Her creativity also extends to art and photography (as seen in this book) as well. She holds a Ph.D in Curriculum and Instruction from the University of Louisville and has been in the teaching field for over 37 years.

Printed in the USA
CPSIA information can be obtained
at www.ICGtesting.com
LVHW060411310524
781840LV00001B/1